OKLAHOMA II

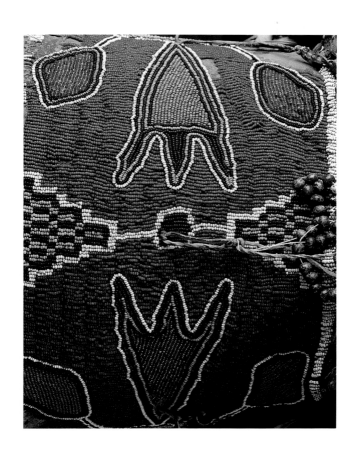

OKLAHOMA II

DAVID FITZGERALD

Essay by George Nigh

GRAPHIC ARTS CENTER PUBLISHING®

To my mother, Lucille, with love.

DAVID FITZGERALD

Without the help of *Oklahoma Today* magazine, the Oklahoma Department of Tourism and
Recreation and all the fine people in the state of Oklahoma, this book would not have been possible.
Special thanks also go to the Oklahoma Historical Society and its curator, Jeffrey Briley.
For over one hundred years, it has been collecting, preserving, and interpreting materials connected with
Oklahoma's history. The images of objects from the State Museum collections provide a glimpse of tangible
objects that now connect us with our history and the diverse cultures that comprise this place.
I would especially like to thank my wife, Mari, for understanding my extended periods of absence.

DAVID FITZGERALD

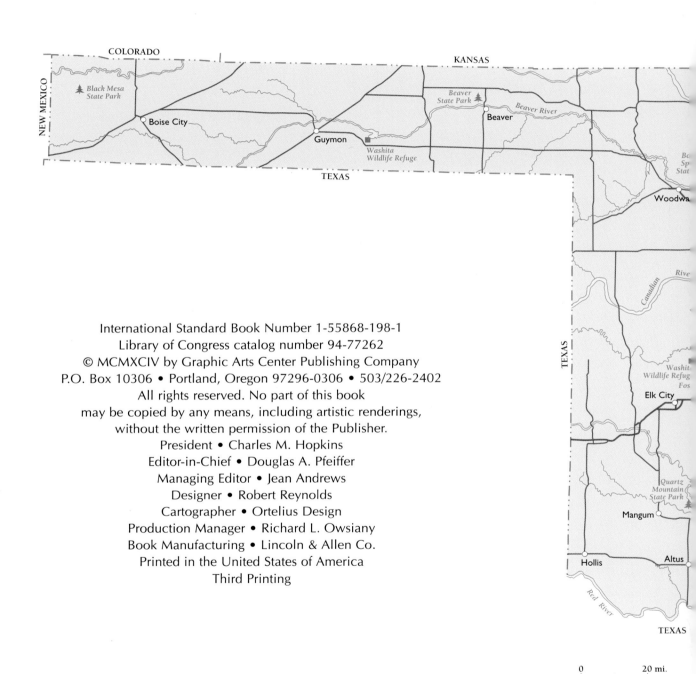

International Standard Book Number 1-55868-198-1
Library of Congress catalog number 94-77262
© MCMXCIV by Graphic Arts Center Publishing Company
P.O. Box 10306 • Portland, Oregon 97296-0306 • 503/226-2402
President • Charles M. Hopkins
Editor-in-Chief • Douglas A. Pfeiffer
Managing Editor • Jean Andrews
Designer • Robert Reynolds
Cartographer • Ortelius Design
Production Manager • Richard L. Owsiany
Book Manufacturing • Lincoln & Allen Co.
Printed in the United States of America
Third Printing

Half Title Page: A Kiowa cradle board, made circa 1895.
Frontispiece: Cascading Travertine Creek flows alongside
mineral and freshwater springs in the Chickasaw National
Recreational Area, established near Sulphur in 1902.

OKLAHOMA

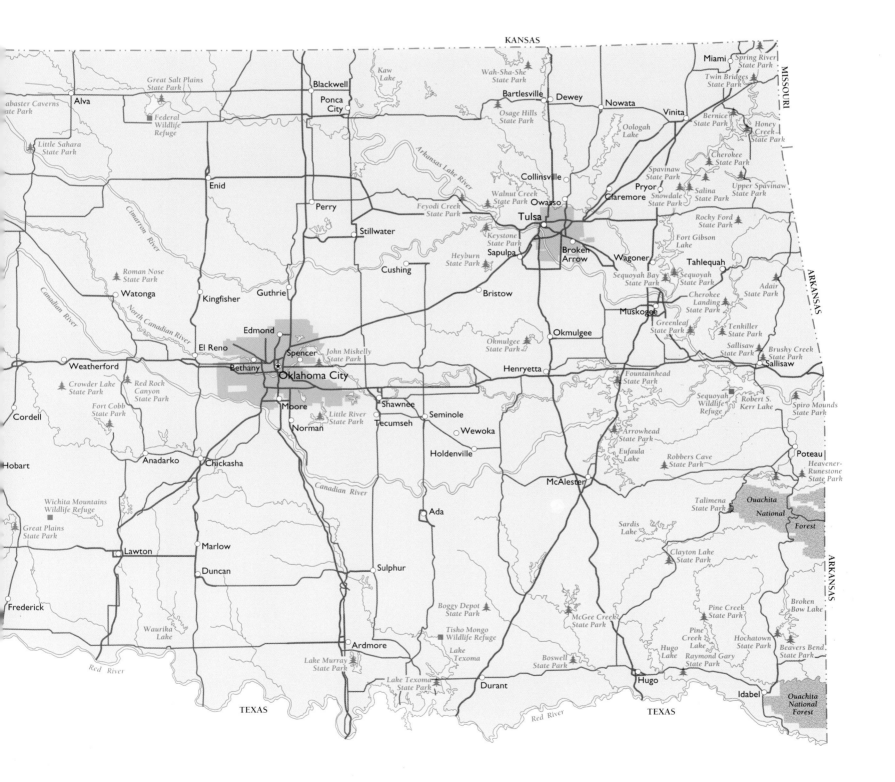

- —— Primary highway
- —— Secondary highway
- ♣ State park
- ■ Wildlife refuge
- ▒ National forest

KANSAS

MISSOURI

ARKANSAS

TEXAS

Alabaster Caverns State Park
Alva
Great Salt Plains State Park
Little Sahara State Park
Federal Wildlife Refuge
Blackwell
Ponca City
Kaw Lake
Wah-Sha-She State Park
Miami
Spring River State Park
Twin Bridges State Park
Bartlesville
Dewey
Nowata
Vinita
Bernice State Park
Honey Creek State Park

Enid
Arkansas River
Lake
Osage Hills State Park
Oologah Lake
Collinsville
Spavinaw State Park
Pryor
Claremore
Salina State Park
Upper Spavinaw State Park
Cherokee State Park

Perry
Feyodi Creek State Park
Walnut Creek State Park
Owasso
Snowdale State Park
Rocky Ford State Park

Stillwater
Tulsa
Keystone State Park
Broken Arrow
Fort Gibson Lake
Tahlequah

Cushing
Heyburn State Park
Sapulpa
Wagoner
Sequoyah State Park
Adair State Park

Roman Nose State Park
Watonga
Kingfisher
Guthrie
Bristow
Sequoyah Bay State Park
Cherokee Landing State Park
Tenkiller State Park

North Canadian River
Cimarron River
Canadian River
Edmond
Okmulgee
Muskogee
Greenleaf State Park
Sallisaw State Park
Brushy Creek State Park

El Reno
Spencer
John Miskelly State Park
Okmulgee State Park
Sallisaw

Weatherford
Bethany
Oklahoma City
Henryetta
Fountainhead State Park
Sequoyah Wildlife Refuge
Robert S. Kerr Lake
Spiro Mounds State Park

Crowder Lake State Park
Red Rock Canyon State Park
Moore
Little River State Park
Shawnee
Seminole

Cordell
Fort Cobb State Park
Norman
Tecumseh
Wewoka
Arrowhead State Park
Eufaula Lake
Robbers Cave State Park
Poteau
Heavener-Runestone State Park

Hobart
Anadarko
Chickasha
Holdenville
McAlester
Talimena State Park
Ouachita National Forest

Wichita Mountains Wildlife Refuge
Canadian River
Ada
Sardis Lake
Clayton Lake State Park

Great Plains State Park
Marlow
Pine Creek State Park
Broken Bow Lake

Lawton
Duncan
Sulphur
Boggy Depot State Park
McGee Creek State Park
Pine Creek Lake
Hochatown State Park
Beavers Bend State Park

Frederick
Waurika Lake
Tisho Mongo Wildlife Refuge
Lake Texoma
Hugo Lake
Raymond Gary State Park

Red River
Ardmore
Lake Murray State Park
Boswell State Park
Hugo
Idabel
Ouachita National Forest

Lake Texoma State Park
Durant
Red River

TEXAS

5

"Crossing the Red" by Harold T. Holden, at Jackson's County Courthouse, was dedicated in honor of pioneers who founded the town of Altus.

EXACTLY WHERE IS OKLAHOMA? Perhaps we first need to determine where it is *not*. It is not out West, down South, up North, back East.

As *Will Rogers,* Oklahoma's most famous citizen, once said, "Oklahoma is the heart, it's the vital organ of our national existence."

We are the meeting point. We are where North meets South and East meets West. We are the heartland, the breadbasket, the backbone of America. We are where this country comes together. We are where it's at!

If you drew a diagonal line over the forty-eight contiguous states from New England to Baja California and another diagonal from the great Northwest to the tip of the Florida Keys, where those lines would cross . . . is . . . somewhere up in Kansas. But we are talking about Oklahoma, so come down just a little . . . there.

Oklahoma's 1994 *Vacation Guide* says, "Barely south of the middle of America, Oklahoma is an ecological crossroads, where eastern and western species of animal and plant life mingle. The Red River carved out the state's southern border; up north, the Cimarron River runs along the length of the Panhandle and cuts across the northwest ridge of the state. Mountains stack up against the eastern border, and a huge swath of tall grass prairie rolls down from the north.

"Nature pours it on in southeastern Oklahoma, with no holds barred. The blue-tinged mountains are thick with towering pines, oak and hickory, with foliage as green as the inside of an emerald. Rivers run wild, rushing across smooth pebbles and collecting mist in the mornings. In Autumn, the Kiamichi Mountains dress in scarlet, brilliant pumpkin and yellow; in Spring in clouds of wildflowers.

"Out in the far western tip of the Panhandle, Black Mesa at 4,973 feet above sea level is Oklahoma's highest point and affords one of the state's best views; you can see all the way into New Mexico [not to mention, on a clear day, with good eyes, Colorado, Kansas, and Texas]. Hikers can follow a trail to the top. Allow four hours [if I'm with you, six]. Even if you don't attempt the summit, scenic landscapes and landmarks abound: a three-state marker where the borders of New Mexico, Colorado, and Oklahoma meet; pastel rock formations; and expanses of cactus, juniper trees, and wildflowers.

"Northeastern Oklahoma is blessed with a little bit of everything: the Ozark Mountains lap over the border of Arkansas in the east, the magnificent Tallgrass Prairie spills over from Kansas borders, scenic rivers run, blue lakes sparkle, and everywhere rolling hills—well, roll.

"In the northeast, there is Tulsa, our second largest city and the Oil Capital of the World. When oil money came gushing into Tulsa in the 1920s, tycoons built luxurious homes but also built for the city's future, erecting not only magnificent office buildings filled with brass and marble, but Art Deco cathedrals and churches, parks, and museums." Tulsa's two fine art museums, Gilcrease and Philbrook, were oil field legacies.

Will Rogers said, "Every realtor should study Tulsa. If your state or city ever strikes oil, you'll know how an oil city should be conducted."

The *Vacation Guide* says "There is as much sky as there is grass in Southwestern Oklahoma—and there's lots of grass. 'The middle and immeasurable meadow of North America' is how Kiowa writer N. Scott Momaday once described this land. There is more to meet the eye than rolling plains, however: the granite boulders of the Wichita Mountains spread across five counties."

Here, in Oklahoma's center, is where I spent thirty-two years of public service at the State

Caddoan artifact from A.D. 750-1450

Capitol in the state capital, Oklahoma City, the largest metropolitan area in the state. At one time, it was the largest city in the world— geographically. Former Mayor Patience Latting used to say she was the largest woman mayor in the world.

Here at the Crossroads of America, there is truly much to do. Look around. Rodeo is big, even in Oklahoma City (along with cowboy hats and boots), and so are painting, poetry readings, Oklahoma City Philharmonic, Remington Park, Kirkpatrick Center, and National Cowboy Hall of Fame and Western Heritage Center. Check out the Air Museum at the Kirkpatrick Center. Here you will visit one of the world's last frontiers where Wiley Post began space travel with his specially designed helmets. (Oklahoma has given the world more astronauts than has any other state.)

Oklahoma is the melting pot of the melting pot. People of all races, colors, creeds, and national origins have come our way, and we are better for it. The Krebs-McAlester coal fields, in my home county of Pittsburg, are a typical example of the fact that we are the melting pot. They opened in 1873 with immigrant miners from England, Ireland, Scotland, and Wales. The Italians followed in 1874; the Lithuanians, in 1875; the Slovaks, in 1883; the French in 1889; and finally the Mexicans. In fact, so culturally diverse were the workers that mine owners are said to have hotly complained about the number of holy days, holidays, fiestas, and national celebrations that interrupted their work force.

WHO WAS HERE FIRST? Who first discovered the land now called Oklahoma? Well, who was here first depends, naturally, upon whom you ask.

We don't call Oklahoma "Native America" for nothing. According to at least one source, we are home to more Native Americans than any other state. The arts and culture of sixty-four tribes add much to the color and fabric of our state. Thirty-seven tribal nations maintain offices in the state. After all, the name itself, Oklahoma, was given to us by the Choctaw leader, Allen Wright. From Wright's native tongue came the words, *okla,* meaning "people," and *humma,* meaning "red."

Who was first? American Indians, period. Case closed. But, of course, as you would expect, there are others who may have also come our way and left their marks, not only figuratively, but literally.

Let's start by remembering some specific dates in our history: in 1492, Columbus sailed the ocean blue; in 1889, unassigned lands were opened for the "run" and settlement; in 1907, statehood was achieved for the forty-sixth state, Oklahoma. I taught history for seven years at McAlester High, so I hesitate to question whether or not Columbus really did discover America— and if I did, my Italian friends at Pete's Place in Krebs would ration my lamb fries and spaghetti.

But according to Bonnie Speer, who wrote *Moments in Oklahoma History,* there might have been many others who came this way.

"Many people believe that the Phoenicians, Libyans, Iberians, Celtics, and Portuguese visited Oklahoma long before the time of Christ. Numerous images of ships have been found carved into stone in the valleys of the Arkansas, Canadian, and Cimarron Rivers. The oldest carving, the Pontotoc Stone in the county by the same name, is dated 500 B.C. Another major carving was discovered in the mesa country near the Oklahoma-Colorado border. Here on a cliff side is a forty-foot panel carved with strange ships and symbols from another century.

"What happened to the residents of the Spiro Mounds in eastern Oklahoma is one of the

Watch used in 1889 Oklahoma land run

Post Oak Lake is one of twelve man-made lakes in Wichita Mountains Wildlife Refuge, near Lawton in Comanche County.

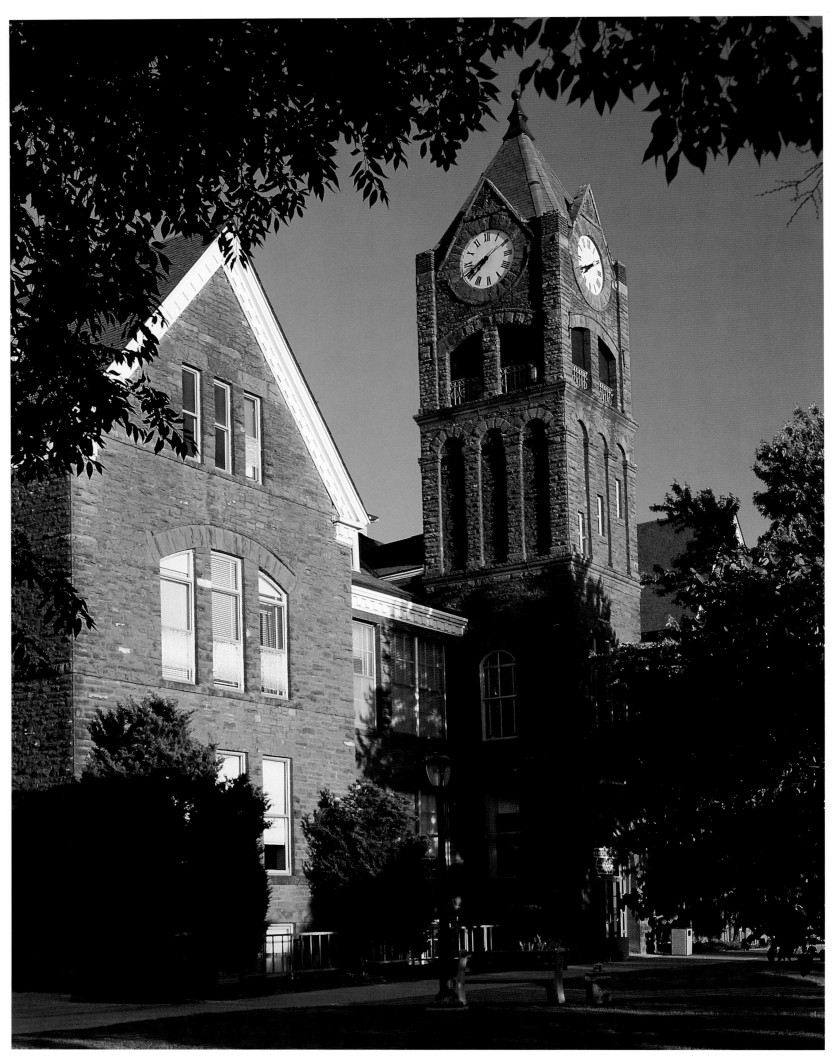

Oklahoma Territory's first higher education building, "Old North Tower," was built in 1891 at the University of Central Oklahoma in Edmond.

great mysteries. From 750 A.D. to 1450 A.D., this site served as an important ceremonial center. Archaeological evidence shows it had highly advanced culture with a sedentary way of life. Village craftsmen produced fine pottery, textiles, sculptures, and metal goods. They established extensive trade routes. Yet by 1450, for some unknown reason, those living here abandoned the site. Only a few priests remained to perform the sacred ceremonies. Soon those left, too.

"Some people believe the Vikings may have been among our state's earliest explorers. For years runeologists studied six strange markings carved on a slab of granite near Heavener. The markings were first discovered by the Choctaws in 1828. It was not until 1969 that a World War II cryptoanalysis expert deciphered the inscription: *November 11, 1012.* His news startled the world. The runestone indicated the Vikings had been here 400 years before the discovery of America by Columbus. Today, the inscription is preserved in the Runestone State Park."

I will not say with certainty who chiseled the markings on the Heavener Runestone, where the visitors came from, or what they were doing, but according to the Tourism and Recreation folks, the slab of stone itself is twelve feet high, ten feet wide, and sixteen inches thick. It tumbled from the surrounding cliffs during some remote geological accident, burying itself in an upright position like a prehistoric billboard.

To date, it is the largest of five runestones found in Oklahoma. Two young boys from Poteau discovered in 1967 a much smaller stone with seven perfectly carved runes. Two months later, the same boys found a missing piece of the same stone with an eighth rune. The date on this stone was exactly five years later than the one of the Heavener Runestone, or November 11, 1017 A.D.

From nuestros amigos (my two years of Spanish finally paid off) to the far south comes word that Cortés and his army in the meantime had conquered the Aztecs and all of Mexico was now a Spanish province, with all the property belonging to Cortés.

Well, said Francisco Vasquez de Coronado, *two can play this game.* Keenly interested in the stories about the rumored seven Cities of Cibola (the seven cities of gold), off he went with his army to the north (remember, he's the one who brought the horses). Through what are today's New Mexico, Colorado, Arizona, and Oklahoma marched the conquistadores in search of the golden treasures. The Oklahoma portion of their trip took forty-two days and lay along what would later become the Chisholm Trail.

Coronado found cities for sure—or at least grass-thatched villages—but no gold and silver. He wrote back that all he found were "humped back cows and flat, black land." Little did he realize that he was a visionary for the great cattle raising area of the plains and the oil that made the land black.

So now we have established the Spanish were the "first white men" in Oklahoma. But how do we know? Well, they kept a written record of their travel, and as they traveled across the Panhandle, the leader's name was left chiseled on Castle Rock, where the future Santa Fe Trail would cross the Cimarron River. Inscribed seventy years *before* the *Mayflower* landed at Plymouth Rock, it stated simply, "Coronatto, 1541."

This has to be proof positive, his name written in stone. But wait, not quite so fast there, amigo. *Coronado* was the leader, and the name that was chiseled on Castle Rock was *Coronatto.* Doubters are quick to point out that *Coronatto* is the Italian, not the Spanish, spelling for Coronado.

Choctaw horn spoon, bowl, and basket

But wait another minute, true believers are equally quick to point out, the outrider for the Spaniards was indeed an Italian, and it was he who left the marker for Coronado to follow.

Who was first? Take your pick.

I'm not putting down any version of who was first. I'm just saying that many diverse cultures have made significant contributions to modern Oklahoma, and we appreciate those folks. As the great philosopher Pogo would say, "they is us."

By the way, those folks were just traveling through. It was the French (wouldn't you know it?) who first settled here, and in the historical "French and Indian" relationship, they traded, settled, and married into the best trading grounds. The most famous and first permanent settlement was situated on the east bank of Grand River in Mayes County on the site of present-day Salina. This trading post was settled by A. P. Chouteau who did quite well trading with John Jacob Astor, and the Chouteaus have remained very prominent in Oklahoma's history.

Will Rogers also believed in trading; however, his advice pertained to stocks, not furs. "Don't gamble, take all your savings and buy some good stocks, and hold it till it goes up, then sell it. If it don't go up, don't buy it."

So the French joined the Indians who were already settled here. Some of the Indians were already here on their own; others had been forced here by the Union Army. Perhaps their hatred for the Blue uniforms explains why most fought on the side of the Gray uniforms, the Confederacy, in the Civil War. In fact, the Cherokee General, Stand Watie, gave up his Confederate forces at Fort Towson, some two months *after* General Robert E. Lee surrendered at Appomattox.

The Indians had been given this new land for "as long as the waters flow and the grass grows green." Somehow, we must have had a major drought long before the *Grapes of Wrath* and the Great Dust Bowl of the Thirties. The United States Government held that treaties with the tribes had been invalidated by their fighting on the side of the South.

Early on, tribal permission was necessary to settle here, but after some promotions by David L. Payne and his Boomers (those who advocate or boom), the United States Government decided to open some of the lands to white settlement.

What a period in history! People, literally from around the world, came that first day on April 22, 1889, to stake their claims on this new frontier. Thousands gathered on the perimeter of the land that was to be opened, and at high noon, cavalry rifles fired the signal to start the run. Thus were born the Eighty-Niners who began carving out Oklahoma Territory. The race was to the fastest, swiftest, and sometimes crookedest. Those who got there first drove a stake with their name on it into the ground, and their life began anew as property owners. At noon on April 22, there was no Oklahoma City, but by sunrise on the 23rd, more than ten thousand people lived in Oklahoma (tent) City.

Of course, not everyone played by the rules. Some hid out under the cover of darkness the night before, waited until they saw someone approaching after the run had started, and then jumped out with their illegal stake as though they had just arrived. These folks got there sooner than the others. Thus was born the nickname, "Sooner State."

The Land Run of 1889 and the opening of the Cherokee Strip, as etched into history by Edna Ferber's *Cimarron,* were the most famous, but Oklahoma was actually settled in fourteen different land runs. After the first five, authorities

Detailed 1895 Kiowa cradle board

Elk Mountain overlooks sunflowers beside Treasure Lake in Charons Garden Wilderness Area in the Wichita Mountains Wildlife Refuge.

13

Lake Altus nestles beneath the Granite Hills in Quartz Mountain State Park, which contains some 29 tree varieties and 140 wildflower species.

decided scrambling for land was too dangerous, caused too many disputes, and resulted in too many deaths. Other methods, including lotteries and auctions, were later employed.

THE SHAPE WE'RE IN. Physically, the state of Oklahoma is easily identifiable—in fact, one of the most identifiable shapes in the Union. Everyone can point out "the pan." But how did the state get this shape?

On November 16, 1907, we became the forty-sixth state, followed by Arizona, New Mexico, Alaska, and Hawaii. But it isn't all that easy to say what we look like, because we were really put together by design on one hand, yet unintentionally on the other.

It started with Twin Territories, Oklahoma and Indian. They are identified as Oklahoma Territory and Indian Territory, O.T. and I.T. for short.

My dad, Wilbur, was a Missouri farm boy who ran away from home in the early 1900s at age fourteen and ended up marrying an Oklahoma girl, Irene, who had been born in Vinita, Indian Territory, in 1899.

In the 1960s, soon after my wife, Donna, and I were married, we were on a trade mission to Germany. We were traveling with a large business group and, of course, as required, we all had our passports. There we were, lined up at the airport, passports and ID's in hand. The German immigration officer looked at our passports and waved us through. That is, except for me. It was a bit embarrassing, since I was the ranking official of the party. He kept thumbing through my passport, checking some kind of list, frowning and motioning me to stay back and for the others to move forward. The trade delegation made all kinds of clever remarks that today would cause any decent airport security to throw us all in prison.

Finally, another German official who barely spoke English came to see what was causing the delay. The two officials exchanged conversation, glances, and puzzled looks. Then I was made aware of a discrepancy on my passport. I, perhaps, could not enter into Germany. In those days, the state of your parents' birth had to be listed on the passport, and German immigration was very puzzled. "We have IA, IND, ILL, but no I.T." They could not admit this impostor from a nonexistent American state. Not to overkill, I gave them an abbreviated version of my "Proud You're an Oklahoman" speech and told about my mother being born in Indian Territory. They waved me through to a rousing round of applause from my fellow travelers.

Meanwhile, we had Twin Territories that were not quite sure they were even pleased to be brothers—one run by Indians, one run by non-Indians. It doesn't take a rocket scientist to figure out that the Indians calculated (correctly) as to how the white settlers were going to want to absorb them. So the Indian Territory held their own separate Constitutional Convention and applied to the Congress of the United States for admission to the Union as the State of Sequoyah in honor of that great Cherokee who had created a written language that enabled his tribe to become the first Native American nation to actually be able to read and write as well as speak in their native tongue.

Now, Congress didn't cotton too much to this. As history records, in the "Great Compromise" of our Constitution, each state gets equal representation in the United States Senate, and if Sequoyah and Oklahoma were accepted as two separate states, there would be *four* new senators. Worse yet—a political nightmare for the Republicans—was the conviction that all four new senators

Early 1800s Colt Paterson "Texas Model"

would probably be Democrats. So, President Teddy Roosevelt, who used to hunt coyotes down around Frederick, said that two Democrats are better than four, so we'll just join the two territories together and create one state.

So it became official on November 16, 1907. The event was celebrated in the then-capital city of Guthrie, in front of the Carnegie Library with the symbolic wedding of Mr. Oklahoma Territory and Miss Indian Territory.

While they were going about admitting this new state, Congress looked a little further to the northwest, and lo and behold, there was a rectangular piece of land afloat out there that literally belonged to no man. It also wanted to join the Union as another separate state of Cimarron. Six senators? Six Democrats? No way, wrong, not. We'll just put you with those other folks from the Twin Territories in Oklahoma.

Texas had just chopped this "No Man's Land" off when they were admitted to the Union, as they couldn't own land north of a certain line and become part of the Union as a "slave state." They deannexed what are now three counties in Oklahoma. This "No Man's Land" later put the handle on the pan—the Oklahoma Panhandle.

During its hey day, No Man's Land not only meant that it did not belong to anyone, it also meant that there was no law. Thus, it became the in-and-out home of numerous gangs, such as Frank and Jesse James, the Dalton Boys, etc. Rob a bank, ride fast to No Man's Land, and wave at the sheriff or marshall when you crossed the line. No problem.

Two additional United States Supreme Court decisions added more land to Oklahoma at the expense, once again, of Texas. One involved a man by the name of Marcy who did the survey for the United States Government after the Louisiana Purchase of 1803, including most of present-day Oklahoma. He was to go up the Red River, as mentioned in the purchase, to a certain point, then cross the river and proceed north. Well, Marcy made one big mistake. He came to a fork in the river and took the wrong one. The correct fork was the main channel, and of course, one always follows the main river, not a tributary.

Because of this surveyor's error, the United States Supreme Court held that what was then Greer County, Texas, belonged to Oklahoma; it became the three Oklahoma counties of Greer, Jackson, and Harmon. Thus, folks like Darryl Royal, the great coach of Texas University, was born an Okie instead of a Texan. Of course, Texas, always wanting to be bigger and better, proudly points out that three counties in Oklahoma were only one county in Texas.

But we didn't stop there in getting all the land we could back from Texas. If you reread about Marcy, you'll notice he was to proceed up the Red River to a certain point, "then crossing the river" to proceed north. This clearly indicated to the highest court of the land that the United States had purchased the land to the south banks of the river, not just to the middle of the channel, which is the usual boundary. Oklahoma owned it all, not just half.

No big deal, you say? The middle of the river or the south bank? Who cares? We do! Just ask the Oklahoma Tax Commission about the oil rights, royalties, and taxes that come from wells drilled in the bed of the Red River.

To summarize: take the Twin Territories, throw in No Man's Land, take the South Fork of the Red River, start on the far south bank, and go north till you touch Kansas, west till you touch Colorado, keep going west until you touch New Mexico, then turn around and go all the way back east till

Outlaw Al Jennings's cowboy boots

Cedar limbs adorn granite boulders in view of King Mountain in Quartz Mountain State Park, popular for its recreational options.

The Granite Hills of Quartz Mountain State Park rise up from Greer County's vast wheatland. One of Oklahoma's largest industries is agriculture.

you reach Missouri, turn south to Arkansas and keep going to the Red River, and you've got OKLAHOMA—and we're in a great shape.

PLACE NAMES. Our place names tell a great deal about our heritage. Many names are clearly in honor of Indians or Indian tribes and nations. A great number of names of communities were given by railroad employees from around the world as they laid the rails and worked the mines. Some will tell you of our settlers' heritage before they came to the territories. Naturally, many honor territorial, state, and national public officials and personalities.

We have Ada, the county seat of Pontotoc, named for Ada Reed. She was the daughter of the first postmaster, William J. Reed.

Afton is named for the river in Scotland; Agra comes from India; and Algiers takes its name from the city by that name in North Africa.

Arkoma combines Arkansas and Oklahoma; Texoma is derived from Texas and Oklahoma.

Big Cedar is known, not for how it received its name, but for an event that took place long after it received its name. It is a one-service-station crossroads, so size is not a factor in its "fame." In the early 1960s, President John F. Kennedy came to dedicate a national scenic highway. Every politican from four states joined a huge crowd to hear at least twenty speakers say how great it was to have this President of the United States at Big Cedar to cut the ribbon. After all that talking—guess what?—*they forgot to cut the ribbon!* But the Talimena Drive, which goes from Talihina, Oklahoma, to Mena, Arkansas, is still there and offers some of the most spectacular fall foliage in Oklahoma.

The town of Gene Autry, in Carter County, was once known as Berwyn. Its name was changed to Gene Autry on January 1, 1942, in honor of the motion picture singing cowboy. Gene Autry was a railroad station agent, and according to folklore, was sitting on the dock one day at Berwyn strumming his guitar and singing when Will Rogers made a stop coming through on the train. Will supposedly told Gene he ought to be in pictures, and if he ever got to Hollywood to look him up. He did! And all the time he was singing, "Make the San Fernando Valley My Home," he was buying up the land.

Waukomis is believed to be a modification of "walk home us," which comes from a time when railroad officials had to walk back to Enid.

Slapout comes from a tale where the local storekeeper always replied that he was "slapout" of whatever item was requested.

CELEBRATIONS. Oklahoma's celebrations are many. As *Will Rogers* once said, "Every town should have some kind of yearly celebration. Didn't Rome have its annual bathing festival? So, think up something for your town to celebrate. Have a parade. Americans all love a parade. Oklahoma has all kinds of various 'weeks,'—'Eat an Apple Week' and 'Don't Cuss the Republicans Any More Than You Can Help Week.'" But Claremore, Oklahoma, home of the great radium water, has one of the most practical and useful ones, "Take a Bath Week."

"Every holiday ought to be named 'Labor Day,'" is another great quotable by *Will Rogers.* "If we could ever get vacation down to where you wasn't any more tired on the day one was over than on our regular work day it would be wonderful." Well, I guess those folks in the town of Canadian got the message 'cause they celebrate "Labor Day No Work Weekend."

It works for them.

Native American western cowboy gloves

I recently spoke to the Warr Acres Chamber of Commerce, and coincidentally, my message was directed to this concept. I feel strongly that every community, town, city, metropolis, or region should come together on any concept that pulls everyone together. Be it serious or funny, we all need something to celebrate and underscore that local spirit. Sometimes the lighter side is the more successful. Beaver brings worldwide attention to their annual Cow Chip Throwing contest. Stroud began its annual world champion Brick Throwing contest for the men several years ago, with Stroud, England, and Stroud, Australia. Recently, in order to be politically correct, the town added a women's competition in Rolling Pin throwing.

However, it is Wetumka that may have made the most out of nothing. Every year in August, thousands come to Wetumka to celebrate a non-event. Years ago, some out-of-state con men came to town in advance of a circus that was to follow. They ordered all the trimmings from area businesses and, of course, sold advertising in the program. The big day came, but the circus didn't. No elephants, no clowns, no flying trapeze. What was there? Just all the trimmings for hamburgers and lots of people. So what did they do? They went ahead with their party. And thus was born the annual "Sucker Day."

Oklahomans celebrate everything: Bald Eagle Town, Muzzle Loading, Bullnanza at the Lazy E (Guthrie), Fall Foliage, Hay Days (Inola), Hog Calling Contest (Weatherford), Rattlesnake Hunts (Okeene/Mangum), Italian Festival (McAlester), Chocolate Festival (Norman), Brick and Rolling Pin Festival (Stroud), All Night Singing (Hugo/Konawa), Red Earth (Oklahoma City). One of the greatest events in the United States—no, make that the world—and two of my personal favorites

among the myriad other festivals and celebrations are the Grapes of Wrath Festival (Sallisaw) and Whole Hawg Day (Eufaula). The Grapes of Wrath Festival is a celebration of John Steinbeck's *Grapes of Wrath* where he traced the Joads and all other "Okies" to California. As *Will Rogers* once said (or did he?) "It raised the I.Q. level of both states."

You will find many things to your liking in every area, in every month. It could be a private or public event or facility. Many of our state-owned resort areas also host events.

As a former Lieutenant Governor who served as the chairman of the Oklahoma Tourism and Recreation Commission, let me suggest that you visit some of our sixty-one state parks and all of our five outstanding state resorts. In addition, be sure to visit our privately owned resorts. Sail on our beautiful (all man-made) lakes and see what we learned about conservation, flood control, industry and tourism, fishing, and sailing. Be sure to SEE and (water) SKI OKLAHOMA! We've got more shoreline miles than either the Pacific or the Atlantic coasts.

As *Will Rogers* once said, "There ought to be a law against anybody going to Europe till they had seen the things we have in this country."

It is impossible to be in Oklahoma very long before becoming aware that the lure and lore of the West are still the most important parts of our life. We have previously mentioned our great rodeos, so let's discuss the other half of our Western heritage.

The Native Americans in Oklahoma celebrate their culture in numerous ways. One of the most colorful demonstrations of tradition is the powwow. The contemporary intertribal powwow is a gathering of many tribes, coming together for the purpose of singing, dancing, feasting, selling and

Roosevelt's pen making Oklahoma a state

Dedicated in 1894, "Old Central" was the first permanent building on the campus of what is now Oklahoma State University.

Will Rogers, "Oklahoma's favorite son," was born in this house. Built in 1875, it was moved a mile west in 1959 to make way for Lake Oologah.

trading arts and crafts, and upholding traditional customs. You particularly will want to visit Red Earth Festival, held every spring. In my opinion, it is one of the great events.

Visitors are welcome at intertribal powwows, although courtesy dictates that all guests remain watchful and respectful. Spectators should not sit on benches encircling the area or take flash photography during the contests. It is polite to ask dancers and singers for permission before taking their pictures.

Guests may join the dance during the Round Dance or at the invitation of the emcee. Guests may also enter the dance floor to participate in a "Giveaway." It is important to remember the dance area is sacred. Out of respect, women should wear shawls in the dance area. The Round Dance is performed by facing the center of the arena in a large circle. All the dancers circle left while keeping time with the drum. The Giveaway is based on the ancient practice of sharing one's personal success with others.

We generally think of the American West as cowboys and Indians, always with horses. Our image could be a buffalo hunt, the Overland Stage, the Pony Express, the Chisholm Trail, the Santa Fe Trail, or the United States Cavalry at one of our several forts. Always the horse.

As *Will Rogers* once said, "A man that don't have a horse, there is something the matter with him." However, Oklahoma does seem to sport a certain number of us who are "drug store" cowboys. These are people who dress like cowboys, talk like cowboys, walk like cowboys, but they lack the requisite horse.

However, horses are certainly plenteous. A rodeo or similar event goes on at the Lazy E Arena between Guthrie and Edmond seemingly nonstop. But that could be said of Oklahoma City

and the state's seventy-seven counties. Whether it is riding, roping, or racing, we get 'em. Everyone who visits Oklahoma seems to enjoy a rodeo or the racing at Oklahoma City's Remington Park or Sallisaw's Blue Ribbon Downs.

However, horses were not always part of the American West. Remember Cortés, that Spanish Conquistador? He and his Spanish brothers were the ones who first brought the horse to America. When the Indians fought the advancing soldiers, both sides obviously had casualties; when the Spanish soldiers fell off their horses, the horses ran off into the hills and plains, and thus began the American horse herds. They felt right at home on the prairies where the buffalo roamed.

OKLAHOMA POLITICS. All of the runs and subsequent settlements and livelihoods brought varied political opinions to our state. The northern section was influenced by the Republican wheat growers of the Kansas plains. The southern section along the Red River was influenced by the Democrat cotton growers of Texas. The eastern folk live in "Lapland," the area "where Arkansas laps over into Oklahoma," and the Panhandle folks sometimes think the "downstaters" feel the "handle" is still No Man's Land.

Oklahoma came into the Union during the height of the Populist Movement, the original "power to the people" folks. We didn't really want any elected official to have any power, and we set about to make sure they didn't. We adopted the "weak governor" theory (no personal reflection intended).

The United States Constitution covering the whole country is quite succinct; in contrast, the Oklahoma Constitution is reputed to be the longest of that of any of the other forty-nine states. During ratification in 1907, it took eighteen hours

Wiley Post's Lockheed Vega instruments

to read, and as one of my opponents once said, "and nobody's read it since."

Although Oklahoma has had other colorful and influencial political leaders over the years, none has been more colorful than Governor Bill Murray, "Alfalfa Bill."

I quote from *Native America*, which explains: "Nothing, it seems happened in early Oklahoma politics without 'Alfalfa Bill' Murray taking center stage. Murray, a Tishomingo lawyer, surfaced first at the 1905 Sequoyah Convention, which aimed for separate statehood for Indian Territory. (He was married to the niece of a Chickasaw governor.) Murray also presided over the state's constitutional convention, served as the first state legislature's Speaker of the House and as a United States Representative, and in 1930, after a stab at establishing a colony in Bolivia, was elected Governor of Oklahoma.

"Murray's true claim to fame, however, was his singular personality and unconventional points of view, which he expressed bluntly. He once wired a message to the Supreme Court after it handed down a decision he disagreed with, 'my compliments to the Court. Tell them to go to hell!'

"Governor Murray called out the Oklahoma National Guard no less than thirty-two times— once to close toll bridges across the Red River, once to shut down Oklahoma oil wells in order to drive up the price of oil, and once to stop county-sponsored sales of farms that farmers were unable to pay their property taxes on.

"In 1932, Murray anounced his candidacy for President, against Franklin D. Roosevelt, but failed to get the nomination from the Democratic Party. He died . . . in 1956, but not before he had one more public victory. In 1951 he swore in his son, Johnston Murray, as Oklahoma's governor."

This was our only father-and-son Governor team. As a young legislator from Pittsburg County in the early fifties, the first Governor I served with was the son, Johnston. "Alfalfa Bill" had continued to be the eccentric character he had been all along. He would sit outside his son's Governor's office and autograph, for a fee, controversial books he had written. He continued to wear a handkerchief hanging inside the shirt collar, so his shirt wouldn't get dirty, and he still chewed tobacco, which was his trademark.

To say that he was a brilliant man of the people would be an understatement. One indication of his bonding with the folks was that, during his term as Governor at the height of the Great Depression, the poor were allowed to garden on assigned plots of land at the Governor's house.

It is a toss-up as to who has been our most powerful politician on the national level, but two of the most eligible candidates are Robert S. Kerr (Ada and Oklahoma City), a former Governor and United States Senator, and Carl Albert (Bugtussle and McAlester), a former Congressman from the Third Congressional District and Speaker of the United States House of Representatives. Both had unofficial titles that indicated their stature. Robert Kerr was called "the uncrowned King of the Senate." Presidents got passed in Congress what he let them have. Carl Albert was known as "the Little Giant from Little Dixie." As the Speaker of the United States House, he was only a heartbeat from the Presidency himself when there were vacancies twice in the office of the Vice President. They are my Oklahoma political heroes.

Like the other forty-nine states, Oklahoma has interesting political trivia. In 1966, at age 26, Jed Johnson Jr. (Chickasha) became the youngest Congressman up to that time ever to be elected to the United States House of Representatives.

Otoe eagle talon necklace, Red Rock

Roman Nose State Park was named for Cheyenne Chief Henry Roman Nose, whose tribe chose 160 acres here to fulfill their allotted land.

Mountain Fork River reflects cypress trees. The river crosses Beavers Bend Resort State Park and includes Broken Bow Reservoir.

J. Howard Edmondson, at age 33, of Muskogee and Tulsa became the youngest Governor in the nation in 1958.

Henry Bellmon of Billings, our first Republican Governor, is the only Oklahoman ever elected Governor twice in non-consecutive terms. He was first elected Governor in 1962, then United States Senator in 1968, and then was reelected Governor in 1986.

Henry S. Johnston of Perry was impeached and removed as Governor in March 1929, only to be elected later to the State Senate, where he served with those who had kicked him out.

Mabel Bassett was elected in 1922 to statewide office without ever having voted for herself. (Women couldn't vote.)

In 1990, when J. C. Watts (Eufaula) was elected to the Corporation Commission, he became the first Black Oklahoman of either party elected to a statewide office.

In 1990, David Walters of Canute became the first person ever elected Governor of Oklahoma who lived west of Oklahoma City.

In 1907, Thomas P. Gore of Lawton (related to Vice President Al Gore) was the first blind person ever elected to the United States Senate.

It was my personal privilege to have known or served with the vast majority of Oklahoma office holders. We became a state in 1907. I was first elected to public office in 1950 and left in 1987, so in one role or another, I have been involved with some great public service with men and women of all races from all areas of our state from both political parties.

As *Will Rogers* once said, "I don't belong to an organized political party. I'm a Democrat."

I proudly served in elected office. Many—in fact most—of our elected officials are dedicated public servants. I salute those brave souls who participate in democracy and who will run and serve. I am proud of my career in public office, just as I am proud today to be the President of the University of Central Oklahoma in Edmond. I'm doing my best to prove *Will Rogers* wrong when he said, "Once a man wants to hold a public office, he is absolutely no good for honest work."

Will Rogers also once said, "Oklahoma has the greatest wild west performers in the world. We have produced more ropers and less cabinet members than any state in the Union." But we made progress in that area when Patrick J. Hurley of Coalgate became Secretary of War in the Hoover Cabinet.

Another Oklahoma first was when President Harry Truman appointed Oklahoma native Perle Mesta as the Ambassador to Luxembourg, making her America's first female ambassador. She has two other claims to fame: the Irving Berlin musical, *Call Me Madam,* was about her life; and her maiden name was Skirvin, as in the hotel her father owned in Oklahoma City.

Jeane Kirkpatrick (Duncan) was privileged to serve as United States Ambassador to the United Nations for President Reagan.

Jim Jones (Muskogee and Tulsa), at twenty-five years old, was the youngest person at the time, under Lyndon Johnson, to serve as Chief of Staff at the White House. He later became Congressman for the Second Congressional District and is now the United States Ambassador to Mexico.

William Crowe (Oklahoma City), a former Admiral and Chairman of the Joint Chiefs of Staff for President Bush, is now the United States Ambassador to Great Britain, by appointment of President Clinton.

Ed Corr (Edmond and Perry) served as the United States Ambassador to Peru, Bolivia, and El Salvador under Presidents Reagan and Bush.

Small tomahawks used by Oklahoma tribes

Of course, there are others, and of course, there will be more in the future. And don't forget my interest in being Counsel General in Puerto Vallarta—but only for the months of January and February.

STATE EMBLEMS. Oklahoma's official state emblems will help you to better understand our history and culture. Some of them may seem a little strange to you, but they are official. They were so designated because it meant something important to somebody.

State Seal. Centered by a five-pointed star, each ray contains the seals of the Five Civilized Tribes. In the center of the star are an Indian and pioneer shaking hands under a figure holding balanced scales, representing Justice. The central star is surrounded by forty-five smaller stars representing the other states admitted to the United States before Oklahoma.

State Flag. The basic design is an Osage warrior's buckskin shield, decorated with pendant eagle feathers on a field of blue. In crossed positions over the shield are an Indian peace pipe and the white man's symbol of peace, an olive branch.

I knew the lady who designed the state flag, and Donna and I have an original painting she did of the flag, which she gave to us when we lived in the Governor's Mansion. The Tenth Legislature, in 1925, adopted Mrs. Fluke's design, selected in a contest sponsored by the Oklahoma Society of Daughters of the American Revolution. The original flag did not have the name "Oklahoma" on it; that was added later by the legislature. Mrs. Fluke was a grand lady and an original by her of her design of the state flag is a cherished possession of this Oklahoma booster.

State Wildflower. Indian blanket is a red and yellow flower symbolizing Oklahoma's scenic beauty as well as the state's rich Indian heritage. The full bloom period is in late June and July.

State Floral Emblem. Mistletoe grows on trees throughout the state and is particularly bountiful in the southern regions of Oklahoma. There are those who are opposed to having a parasite as an emblem. I certainly can understand that concern, just as I understand concerns some folks have about the state song having the words "pertaters" and "temayters." But as a student and teacher of history, I realize those things are a part of us. In the same way, it does no good to continue to fret over John Steinbeck in *The Grapes of Wrath* giving us a moniker of "Okies" that will be with us forever.

The mistletoe is a parasite. But during those territorial winters, it was virtually the only living plant available that could be used for funerals. Its dark green leaves and white berries, which show up brightly during the fall and winter in trees that have shed their own leaves, were the floral arrangement on many a casket. My attitude is that if it was good enough for our pioneer forefathers, it's good enough for me. During my years as an elected official, I have had a hand in saving the mistletoe as an official emblem.

State Tree. The redbud grows in the valleys and ravines of Oklahoma. In early spring, its reddish-pink blossoms brighten the landscape throughout the state.

State Rock. Found in Central Oklahoma, the Barite Rose Rock is a reddish brown stone that resembles a rose in full bloom. An old Cherokee legend says the rocks represent the blood of the braves and the tears of the maidens who made the courageous "Trail of Tears" journey in the 1800s to Oklahoma.

State Animal. The American buffalo (or bison) is a massive animal that weighs anywhere from eight hundred to two thousand pounds and stands

Comanche and Cheyenne N. A. church fans

In the heart of the Arbuckle Mountains, the eloquent seventy-seven-foot Turner Falls is a favorite swimming hole and picnic spot.

Oklahoma's first lake built strictly for recreation purposes is in Elephant Rock Recreation Area, situated in Lake Murray State Park.

nearly six feet high at the shoulders. Its large head, a high hump on its shoulders, and shaggy hair toward the front of the body characterize the buffalo.

State Bird. The scissor-tailed flycatcher is a somewhat quiet bird with beautiful plumage and a long, sleek tail (twice as long as its body) that resembles a pair of scissors.

State Motto. The Latin words, *Labor Omnia Vincit,* meaning "Labor Conquors All Things."

State Musical Instrument. The fiddle.

State Song. "Oklahoma," from the Rodgers and Hammerstein musical, *Oklahoma!*

State Fish. White bass, also called sand bass.

State Reptile. Mountain boomer, also called collared lizard.

State Salute. "I salute the flag of the State of Oklahoma. Its symbols of peace unite all people."

As some of you know, I have a show on OETA public television, called *Oklahoma, Yesterday, Today, and Tomorrow.* Recently, I have had several telephone conversations with another grand lady, Mrs. Delphia Warren, of Muskogee, who wrote the official pledge to the flag, in order to arrange to do a television segment interview with her to discuss the pledge and how she came to write it.

Other official state emblems include: Colors, green and white; Country Song, "Faded Love"; Dance, square dance; Flag Day, November 16; Furbearer, raccoon; Game Bird, wild turkey; Game Animal, white-tailed deer; Meal, okra and chicken fried steak (we can't be all bad); Grass, Indian grass *(Sorghastrum nutans)*; Nickname, Sooner State; Monument, Golden Driller, in Tulsa; Pin, the "OK" pin; Poet Laureate, Maggie Culver Fry; Poem, "Howdy Folks"; Soil, port silt loam; Theater (pardon me, it's "theatre"), the Lynn Riggs Players; Waltz, "Oklahoma Wind."

I can actually pinpoint the exact day I first sensed a state pride bursting in my chest. It was the summer of 1943. I was attending McAlester High School. World War II was at its height. High school students had no cars, and if they could manage one, gas was rationed, so you really couldn't go very far. Of course, to further date me into the Dark Ages, there was also no television. So . . . radio was it. The Lucky Strike Hit Parade was the ultimate for any teenager, and jitterbugging was the in thing. I was no exception. The radio was for me.

I remember it was an afternoon, and not my usual evening listening period. I was upstairs on the back porch listening to the box when I became aware that they were singing about *my* state. They were exuberant about *my* state. This electrifying excitement made me proud as for the first time I heard a song called "Oklahoma." No, not *a* song, *the* song "Oklahoma," and my life basically was charted: I, George Nigh, was destined in some form or fashion to be a first-class booster, enthusiast, and cheerleader for my state. I was hooked. I've never forgotten that summer.

So there I was in 1943, listening to this song, little realizing that—just ten short years later, as a McAlester High School Oklahoma History teacher and an elected member of the Oklahoma House of Representatives—I would author the bill that would make that song from this Broadway production our state song. It was great to correspond with Rodgers and Hammerstein and to later attend the Hollywood premiere of the movie *Oklahoma!,* the first movie filmed in Todd-A-O for the wide screen.

The greatest—literally the most recognized—song in captivity, "Oklahoma" is truly heard "round the world." Somewhere in my memoirs is a letter written to then-Governor Johnston Murray

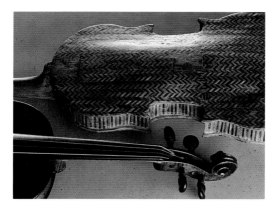

Fiddle, Oklahoma state musical instrument

from a Frenchman who said he had never been to America. But, he said, if he ever came, he was coming to Oklahoma because that is what all the American servicemen sang about in France.

At the previous New York premiere of the movie, Governor Raymond Gary took a bit of Oklahoma soil, raised the state flag over the theater, and claimed it as part of Oklahoma. All those New Yorkers in their black ties had to "walk across Oklahoma" to get inside the theater. To add a little more color, the famous actor, Chill Wills, made all the ladies walk under the mistletoe, and, as is custom, he gave a peck on the cheek to all his "kissin' cuzins."

Ridge Bond (who grew up in McAlester with my older brothers, Bill and Sam, and now lives in Tulsa) is the only Oklahoman ever to have starred in the Broadway production of *Oklahoma!* He was the star, he was Curly, and he was good. (He helped me make this the state song.) He told me this story.

Rodgers and Hammerstein, that dynamic duo of show business, had purchased the rights to an Off-Broadway production called "Green Grow the Lilacs," written by Lynn Riggs (Claremore). They took his already great book; added music and lyrics; hired the legendary Agnes DeMille to be the choreographer; and went about making, breaking, and setting musical history with this fabulous production. It revolutionized musical theater as the first musical production to use the music and dance to help tell the story. Previously, the plot would just stop in the middle of the act, sing or dance, then start up again where it had left off. But not *Oklahoma!* Music and dance were the important part of the story.

As is customary, it opened out of town to iron out the kinks, to get the bugs out, to get it ready for the critics. No one knew how great it would be.

The name was a problem, "Green Grow the Lilacs" became "Away We Go," but they still were not happy; it just didn't have it. They decided that you judge a book by its cover and that neither of the two previously mentioned names captured the enthusiasm of this revolutionary show. They kicked around several other suggestions and had thrown in and thrown out *Oklahoma,* saying it did not capture the punch, the excitement, the enthusiasm they wanted. It didn't quite have the spark they felt was captured on stage. They were beginning to sense the dynamics of the production.

Change the name . . . was the decision, and so they did. The name of this magnificent story about the days from territory to statehood, got a name different from *Oklahoma.* You may be doubting me at this point, but according to Ridge Bond, someone said, let's put an exclamation point after it and call it *Oklahoma!* As Paul Harvey (Tulsa) says, "That's the 'rest of the story." And the rest is history. *Oklahoma!* changed the course of musicals forever. Ever since, we Oklahomans have been doing to our state what two Broadway producers who had never been here did for us: add an exclamation point! And we're doing fine!!!

THOSE !!! Many Oklahomans have been adding their own personal exclamation points to our state with their outstanding achievements. Some are native-born; some stayed for a while as they passed through. Pick any field or profession, and Oklahomans are at or near the top.

One day while he was sitting on his porch with two Texans, Comanche Chief Quanah Parker watched as a star-studded military vehicle with an officer pulled up. Later, he asked the men about the stars on the vehicle and was told they indicated the officer was the leader of many warriors.

A pipestone pipe used by Oklahoma tribes

Sugar maple fall foliage peeks through pine boughs at Clayton Lake State Park in the Kiamichi Mountains.

33

Black Mesa, at 4973 feet, is Oklahoma's highest point. It is in the Panhandle, near the New Mexico and Colorado boundaries.

Shortly thereafter, fourteen white stars appeared on the red roof of Quanah's home; his "Star House" is at Eagle Park near Cache.

Two—both Native Americans, both selected as the best by others—received unusual honors. Jim Thorpe, Sac and Fox Indian from Yale, was the first ever to win both the decathlon and the pentathlon at the Olympics. He was voted by the sports writers as the "World's Greatest Athlete" of the first half of this century. I was honored to be an aggressive supporter in the finally successful effort to have all of Jim Thorpe's medals returned to his family after he had been stripped of them for having played pro baseball one summer.

A Cherokee from Oologah and Claremore, *Will Rogers* was at the same time the world's number one attraction on radio, in newspapers, on stage, and in the movies. Incredible for a cowboy philosopher, humorist, rope-twirling, yarn-spinning, gum-chewing, head-scratching guy. Will was voted the "World's Greatest Humorist" in the first half of this century. It was my pleasure to be co-chair, along with movie actor Joel McCrea, of the international celebration of the life of *Will Rogers.*

Both men made us proud. Jim Thorpe was a quiet man whose physical actions were his words. *Will Rogers,* on the other hand, had much to say about anything or anybody. In fact, it is quite common in Oklahoma today, sixty years after his death, to hear a conversation begin with the phrase, *"as Will Rogers once said."*

Tune in to any Country Music awards program, and enjoy with us the proud feeling of Oklahoma talent. In fact, on just one single national awards program, of the five nominees, four were from Oklahoma—Garth Brooks, Reba McIntyre, Vince Gill, and Dunn of Brooks and Dunn.

These and others from Oklahoma continuously dominate the many nominations and awards.

Our folks put Western in Country and Western. Other names that also stand out are Conway Twitty, Gene Autry, Sammy Smith, Joe Diffee, Roy Clark, Jody Miller, Jimmy Wakely, Wanda Jackson, and Norma Jean.

Music in any area has always been blessed by our abilities in writing, arranging, or performing. The world enjoys the talents of numerous musicians from Oklahoma: Sandi Patty, Roger Miller, Jimmy Webb, Patti Paige, Leon Russell, and—the one guy who may have started it all—Woody Guthrie. Who can deny that this true Okie of the Dust Bowl days is among the truly great song writers, especially the one song "This Land Is My Land, This Land is Your Land."

Hoyt Axton made real toe-tapping music with "Jeremiah Was a Bull Frog," and other great names would include Anita Bryant, John Denver, and my special buddy, Miss Kay Starr.

The stage is no stranger to our performers, whether it be Lynn Riggs, who wrote "Green Grow the Lilacs"; Ridge Bond, star of *Oklahoma!;* Max Wisenhoffer, producer of *Will Rogers Follies;* or, of course, Will Rogers himself.

On November 17, 1991, in the state capitol at Oklahoma City, a mural was dedicated: *Flight of Spirit,* by artist Mike Larsen. This mural was created in honor of Oklahoma's five renowned Native American ballerinas, Yvonne Chouteau, Rosella Hightower, Moscelyne Larkin, Maria Tallchief, and Marjorie Tallchief.

Buy a ticket to the movies, rent a video, or watch television, and on the screen you will see familiar faces: John Forsythe, Jim Garner, Alice Ghostly, Ron Howard, Tony Randall, or Academy Award winners Ben Johnson and Jennifer Jones—all Oklahomans.

No stars shine brighter than our sports figures. Medal winners are John Smith, Mr. Everything in

A random list could start with many Olympic
Jim Thorpe's 1912 Olympic Gold Medals

35

Wrestling; Shannon Miller and Bart Conner, both world champion gymnasts; and Jim Thorpe, the greatest athlete of the first half of this century.

Familiar golf names are David Edwards, Gil Morgan, Doug Tewell, and PGA champions Bob Tway and Orville Moody.

Some of the big names in basketball are Mark Price, Wayman Tisdale, Mookie Blalock, John Starks, Bob Kurland, and—the gentleman of all gentlemen in sports—the great Hank Iba, who capped his coaching career as the coach of the '84 Olympics team.

I have the feeling most people don't realize the baseball giants from our state. For openers, just go back to the '93 World Series. It's the bottom of the ninth, and at bat are the Toronto Blue Jays. The tension mounts, and a home run by Joe Carter wins it all. Other prominent players along the way on various diamonds around the country include Johnny Bench, Bobby Murcer, Allie Reynolds, Warren Spahn, and America's hero, Mickey Mantle.

Football isn't so surprising because of the great power our teams have had these last years. In your mind, turn on your TV set, picture the world champion Dallas Cowboys, and imagine who is fading back for a long touchdown pass. You're right, it's Troy Aikman, the highest-paid player in the NFL. Other names include coaches Bud Wilkinson and Barry Switzer, and many, many many players who have made All-American.

Other names jump out: Dennis Byrd, Thurman Thomas, Keith Jackson, J. D. Roberts, the Selmon Brothers; and of course, Steve Owens, Billy Sims, Billy Vessels, and Barry Sanders all have won the Heisman Trophy.

We are equally excited to talk about our two Miss Americas, Jayne Jayroe and Susan Powell.

Lori McNeil is our tennis star at Wimbledon.

Another lady who has achieved national prominence is Wilma Mankiller. She is the principal chief of the Cherokees and, in 1993, was inducted into the Women's National Hall of Fame.

Rodeo greats include Will Pickett, who was the inventor of bull dogging and recently has had a U.S. postage stamp issued in his honor; and the champion of all champions, Jim Shoulders.

Astronauts include Gordon Cooper, William Pogue, Stuart Roosa, and Owen Garriot. Thomas Stafford commanded the shuttle that linked up with the Russians, and Shannon Lucid has spent more time in space than any other female.

Go shopping, and you'll probably be in retail stores associated with two of our businessmen. W. R. Howell is the CEO of JC Penney, and Sam Walton was the founder of Walmart.

Some of Oklahoma's biggest corporate names would naturally include the oil industry giants of Phillips, Conoco, and Kerr McGee.

In the meantime, "see you in the funnies." Of course, that is *Dick Tracy,* created by Chester Gould; or *Doonesbury,* created by Gary Trudeau.

As you might suspect, I could go on endlessly about Oklahoma. Many more names could be added to this list that is only the beginning. If you are from Oklahoma, I encourage you to mentally make your own list. It is impressive with just the names I have mentioned, but it would be even more so as you add your own.

It is hard to put into words (and probably equally difficult to capture on film) the vibrance of this state. Don't take my word for it; experience the beauty and enthusiasm of OKLAHOMA! It is truly the meeting point, where North meets South and East meets West.

Oklahoma is a meeting of directions, of cultures, a state where events are memorialized and its people stand proud and tall.

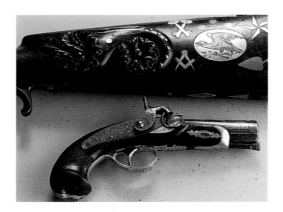

Pistol and rifle stock detail

A majestic mesa rises above Lake Watonga, a fifty-five-acre, fully-stocked artificial lake in Roman Nose State Park.

◄ Tulsa's population of some 367 thousand make it the state's second-largest city, supporting commercial, energy and aviation industries, cultural events, and universities.
▲ Guthrie, Logan County's seat, was Oklahoma's capital until 1910. With sixteen hundred acres of the city listed in the National Historical Register, it has the most complete collection of restored Victorian architecture in the nation.
►► Lake Texoma is behind Denison Dam on the Red River in Texoma State Park. On the boundary between Oklahoma and Texas, the park is popular in both states.

▲ Bartlesville is recognized as a leader in modern archi-
tecture, pioneered by the H. C. Price family. The Santa Fe
Train Depot and Phillip Petroleum Offices are examples.
▶ Cattle graze on the thirty-six-thousand-acre Tall Grass
Prairie Preserve, north of Pawhuska in Osage County.

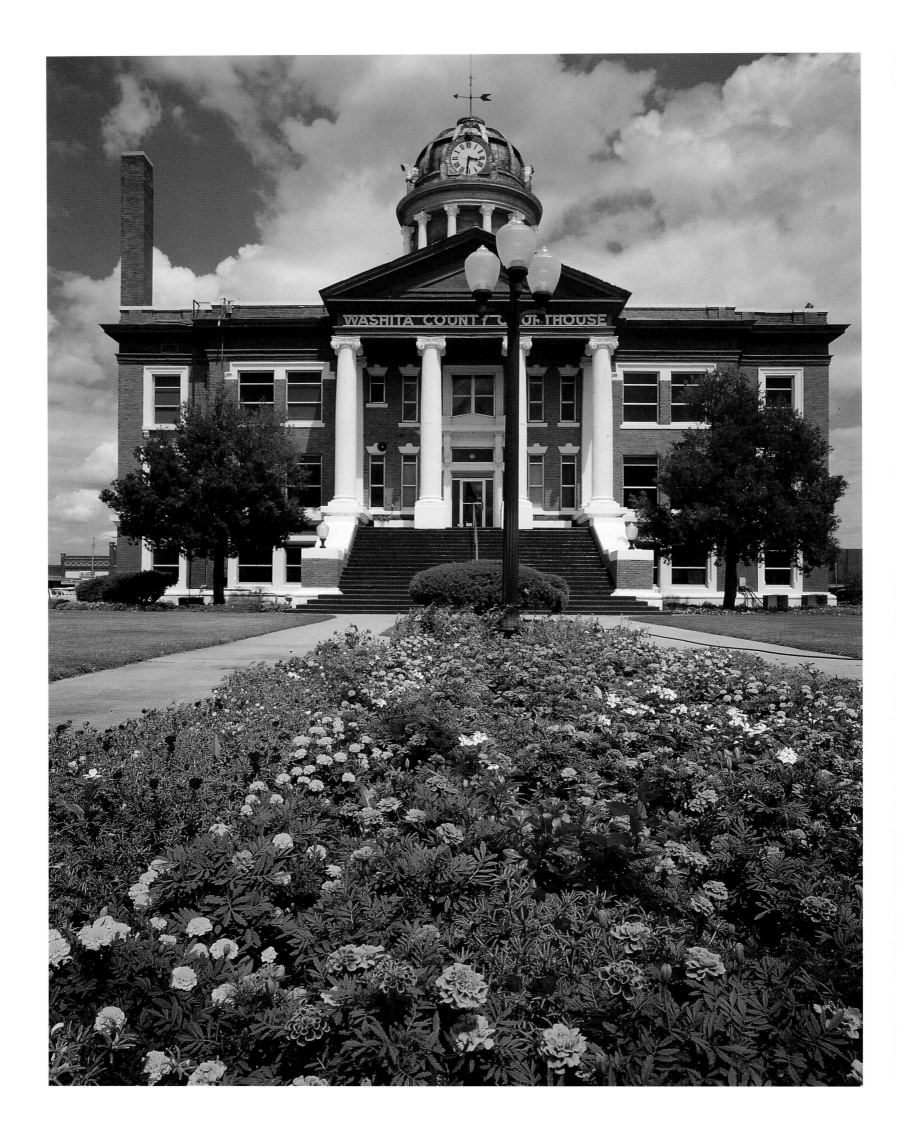

◄ Considered the Father of the Oklahoma courthouses, Cordell Courthouse in Washita County was built in 1910 by the architectural firm of Solomon Andrew Layton.
▲ Near Tahlequah, Chicken Creek Point is a top fishing spot on Tenkiller Ferry Lake, one of Oklahoma's prettiest lakes with 130 miles of shoreline. Around the lake are forested hillsides, steep cliffs, and recreational havens.

▲ The Talimena Scenic Drive, in southeast Oklahoma's
Ouachita National Forest, offers fifty-four miles of mountain views, including Emerald Vista, south of Poteau.
The Ouachita Mountains run an atypical east to west.
▶ The Ouachita National Forest, covering parts of fifteen
counties in Arkansas and Oklahoma, encompasses 1.6
million acres of wilderness, recreation, and water areas.

◄ The popular Broken Bow Lake embodies 14,200 acres
with 180 miles of pine-covered shores in Hochatown State
Park. The lake is situated near the town of Broken Bow.
▲ The Mountain Fork River, which flows through the
3,522-acre Beavers Bend Resort State Park, reflects a few
of the area's tree varieties—both hardwood and cypress.

▲ Shawnee's Santa Fe Depot, built in 1903, is one of the few surviving Romanesque Revival Architectures in the Southwest. In continuous use as a passenger and freight depot until 1973, it opened in 1981 as a museum and is now listed on the National Register of Historical Places.
▶ Sandstone Buttes lies in the far northwest of Oklahoma's Panhandle. Once called "No Man's Land," the Panhandle is about 34 miles wide and 167 miles long. Relinquished by Texas to the United States in 1850, the area was established as Oklahoma territory by the Organic Act of 1890.

◄ In the state's far northwest corner cactus and juniper dot Black Mesa State Park's arid landscape. This environment sharply contrasts the densely forested southeast region.
▲ New Mexico mesas cradle the town of Kenton at the northwest tip of Oklahoma, where mountain time is kept.

▲ North of Pawhuska in Osage County, the Tall Grass Prairie Preserve, some thirty-six thousand acres in all, is now under the protection of the Nature Conservancy.
▶ A small creek lies near the west entrance of the Barnard Ranch, once a working cattle ranch, and now owned and protected by the Nature Conservancy. Buffalo have been brought back to this Tall Grass Prairie Preserve.
▶▶ Sardis Lake, named for Sardis Indian Mission Church, lies northeast of Clayton and southeast of McAlester. The Potato Hills are so named because they look like potatoes.

◄ Capitol Square, situated in the center of Tahlequah, is the restored Cherokee Capitol, which was built in 1870. The drinking fountain memorial was constructed in 1913 to commemorate "Our Confederate Dead" and General Stand Watie, who was the commander of the American Indian Division in 1864 during the War Between the States.

▲ An old chuck wagon, once used on cattle drives, was found by Carl Cooper (left) on Hitch Ranch near Guymon in Texas County. Rick Furnish, Hitch Ranch Manager, is following in his father's forty-four-year managerial career.

▲ Saints Cyril and Methodius Orthodox Christian Church, was established in 1897 in Hartshorne, east of McAlester, by Slavic immigrants from western Russia and eastern Europe. The present church was constructed in 1916.
▶ Sandstone Ridge looks over Lake Carl Etling, an idyllic fishing site in Black Mesa State Park, in the Panhandle.

◄ Forty-nine miles of shoreline envelop the 6,260 acres of
Lake Altus in Quartz Mountain State Park, which was once
a winter campground for the Kiowa and Comanche tribes.
▲ Quartz Mountain State Park is a 4,284-acre preserve
that welcomes boaters, hikers, fishermen, and campers.

▲ The Wichita Mountain Range and 2,464-foot Mount Scott reign over the Wichita Mountains Wildlife Refuge. Texas longhorn and a variety of wildlife—buffalo, wild turkey (the state game bird), white-tailed deer (the state game animal), and others—are protected in the refuge.

▲ Near Konawa, the Bakery is one of the few remaining buildings of the Sacred Heart Mission, which was established in 1875 by the Benedictines. Today, the property is owned and operated by St. Gregory's Abbey and is open to visitors, who enjoy the grounds' twenty-two-acre park.

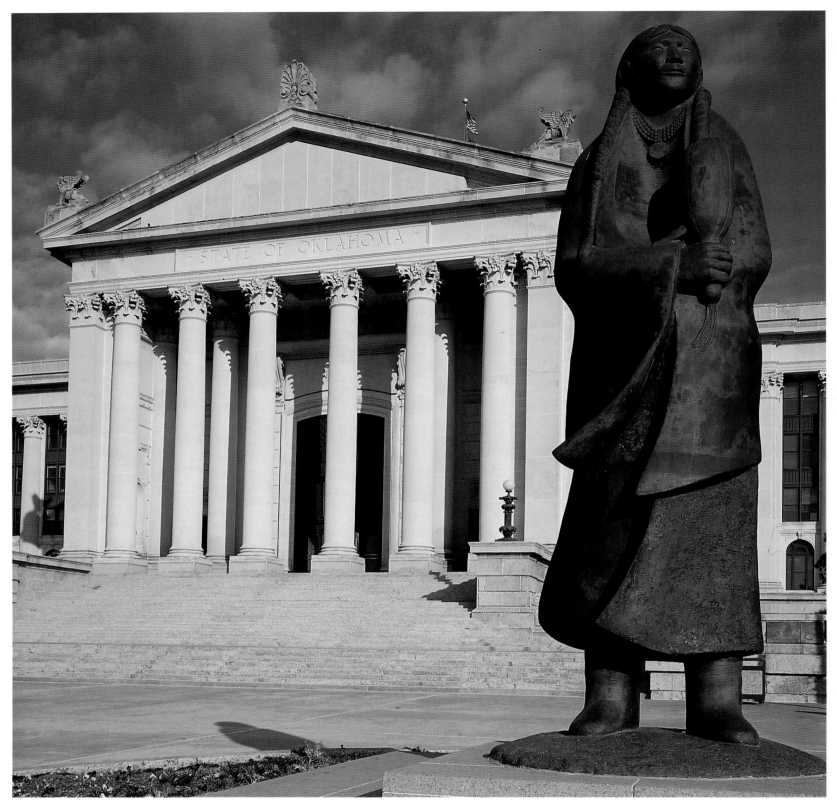

▲ One of the few domeless capitols in the nation, the State Capitol of Oklahoma was completed in 1917. The statue, "As Long as the Waters Flow," was dedicated June 4, 1989. It was created by Allen Houser, a Chiricahua Apache.
▶ Cypress trees line the Mountain Fork River in Beavers Bend State Park, covering some thirty-five hundred acres near Broken Bow. Tennis, water-skiing, and horseback riding are among the many activities available to visitors.

◄ Dunebuggying, motorcycle courses, camping areas, and fishing await the adventurer in Beaver State Park's 377 acres, which range from sand dunes to the Beaver River.
▲ Near Freedom, the red mesas at Alabaster Caverns State Park are surrounded by a large gypsum cave containing alabaster formations, selenite, and several bat species.

▲ The Wichita Mountains Wildlife Refuge, near Lawton, is used as grazelands for Texas longhorn. Bison, also called buffalo, are one of the animals protected in the refuge.
► Backdropped by Rainy Mountain, the ruins of an Indian school, built in the early 1900s, remain on Comanche, Kiowa, and Apache land. N. Scott Momaday's "On the Way to Rainy Mountain" made the mountain famous.
►► In the state's far southeastern corner, cypress trees line the Mountain Fork River. Flowing from Broken Bow Lake in Beavers Bend State Park, the river waters rich forests.

74

◄ Emerald Vista, on Winding Stair Mountain in Ouachita (pronounced WASH-e-ta) National Forest, is only one place to enjoy the scenery along the Talimena Scenic Drive. The rocky, rugged Ouachita Mountains are covered with pine and oak forests and mistletoe, the state flower.
▲ Mountain Fork River is just one example of the million-plus surface acres of freshwater lakes, reservoirs, ponds, rivers, and streams—in a state once called the Dust Bowl.

▲ Civil War soldiers were quartered here in Fort Washita's "West Barracks." Established in 1842 by General Zachary Taylor, the fort was abandoned by Federal forces in 1861 and later occupied by Confederate forces from Texas. Etchings of names and dates are visible on the window.
► Chicken Creek Point lies along Tenkiller Ferry Lake, also called Lake Tenkiller. The lake, covering some 12,900 acres, is situated in the Cookson Hills near Tahlequah.

◄ Cedar Lake nestles in the valley below Winding Stair Mountain in Ouachita National Forest along Talimena Scenic Drive. Three-fifths of the state's southeast quarter is privately owned forest or part of Ouachita National Forest.
▲ Roman Nose State Park offers a wide variety: it is an all-recreation area for campers, anglers, hikers, and picnickers.

▲ In Pushmataha County, Clayton Lake is in the park by the same name. Near the lake is the town of Antlers; according to legend, it was so named because antlers were nailed up at a nearby spring to indicate a campsite.
▶ Oklahoma is proud of its town festivals, which honor anything that comes to mind. In Talihina, near the foot of the Talimena Drive, fall foliage is celebrated each October.

FIRST
PRESBYTERIAN
CHURCH
EST. 1887
Worship Service 11:00

David Marsh

◄ The first service in the Beaver Presbyterian Church on Third Street and East Avenue was held in 1887, and ever since, services have been held regularly in the building.
▲ Oklahoma's First Carnegie Library, was built in 1903 in Guthrie. Frank Frantz (last Territorial Governor) and Charles Haskell (first State Governor) were inaugurated on its steps. In 1908, ninety women made the state flag here.

▲ Clayton State Park in the Kiamichi Mountains is just one of sixty-one state parks. Along with numerous recreational areas and activities, the parks attract millions of visitors, making tourism the second-largest industry in Oklahoma.
▶ Eufaula's building standard on Main Street was a sandstone, pressed-brick, stately edifice with gothic trim. One example is this three-story building, built in 1900 by C. E. Foley. At various times, it has been a bank and a hotel.

◄ Lake Eufaula, Oklahoma's largest with 102,200 surface acres and 600 miles of shoreline, starts from the Canadian River and forms one of the world's largest man-made lakes.
▲ Katy Depot, built in 1908 and used for passenger service until 1965, was placed on the Oklahoma Landmark inventory by the Oklahoma Historical Society in 1980. It is now a Tourist Information Center on Checotah's highways.
►► "Spring of Everlasting Waters" feeds the swimming pool and lake at Roman Nose State Park. The park offers both recreation and superb scenery—resort life at its best.

▲ Goff House, built in 1900 by William and Magdalen Goff, typifies the Colonial Revival and Queen Anne Style. Only 10 percent of homes built in 1900 were of this style.
▶ Lake Eufaula lays claim to the Arrowhead State Park marina. The town of Eufaula was first a Native American village, then a trading post. It is home to the state's oldest continually published newspaper, *The Indian Journal*.

◄ Evalu Ware Russell, who lives near Anadarko, is a full-blood Kiowa and a nationally known story teller. Her buckskin dress—made by her aunt, Anna Saukeah, and cousin, Alma Bigtree—required three years to complete.
▲ Oklahoma's four state hatcheries keep its reservoirs, lakes, rivers, ponds, and streams stocked with catfish, bass, crappie, sunfish, perch, and trout. One recipient of this bounty is Mountain Fork River, in Beavers Bend State Park.

▲ Unique to the Osage tribe, red corn has passed from generation to generation of the Red Corn family. Today, the red corn, which was nearly extinct, has been saved through the efforts of Waltena and Raymond Red Corn, of Pawhuska. Now it will not disappear from the earth.

▲ Oklahoma's state tree, the redbud thrives in valleys and ravines throughout the state just as proudly as the one displayed here in Beavers Bend State Park. For eleven years, in April, Oklahoma City has held the Red Bud Classic (a ten-kilometer run) and the two-mile Fun Walk.

▲ Vanessa Paukeigope Morgan, raised by her Kiowa grandmother, has won National Endowment of the Arts fellowships for her talent in making Kiowa saddles, dolls, buckskin dresses, cradle boards, and fur quivers. Vanessa also contributes to Smithsonian Native American Studies.
▶ Rich Mountain, standing near three thousand feet, is the highest mountain along the Talimena Scenic Drive, in the Ouachita National Forest. Elevations in Oklahoma range from the Little River at 287 feet to Black Mesa at 4,973 feet.

◄ Ardmore Courthouse, built in 1910, is one of seventeen
that were designed by the firm of Solomon Andrew Layton.
▲ The Ouachita National Forest—with its vast expanse of
mountains, water, and trees covering much of west central
Arkansas and southeastern Oklahoma—is a popular desti-
nation for both rugged outdoorsmen and the city slickers.

▲ Lonnie Farley, born in 1916, began his cowhand career at thirteen at the 101 Ranch, then worked thirty-seven years at his uncle's ranch, now the Marchant Ranch. Many ranches later, he is now settled at Valley View's Ranch near Lindsay. He says, "If I sit still I hurt, so I just keep working."

▶ Dogwood blossoms grace the entrance to Beavers Bend State Park on Highway 259A. Abundant in the southeast area, the dogwood prefers the company of other trees.

◄ Cookson Hills, once a popular bandits' hideout, now boasts both a lake and a state park—Lake Fort Gibson and Sequoyah State Park—on the Fort Gibson Reservoir.

▲ Each April since 1967, the 132-acre Honor Heights Park in Muskogee has hosted the Annual Azalea Festival, which offers a parade, art show, garden tours, and entertainment.

►► Oklahoma City, a barren prairie at dawn on April 22, 1889, boomed to a population of approximately ten thousand by nightfall as unassigned land opened to settlement. The city now boasts a population of half a million people.

▲ Mount Sheridan lies on the north boundary of Wichita Mountains Wildlife Refuge above the town of Mears.
► The delicate beauty of Price Falls offers a haven for relaxation in the eastern area of the Arbuckle Mountains.

◄ Mountain Fork River, flowing through Mountain Fork Park, lies two miles south of Beavers Bend State Park. ▲ In the Ouachita National Forest, near the town of Bokhoma, pine trees seem to reflect a forest the early pioneers saw as endless. Today, it shows the state's on-going efforts to preserve what was once taken for granted.

▲ In southeast Oklahoma, the fog and humidity contrast the Panhandle's drier climate. The southeast's average annual temperature is 61°; precipitation, 52 inches. The northwest's temperature is 56°; precipitation, 21 inches.
► Cedar Lake covers eighty-four acres below Talimena Scenic Drive in Ouachita National Forest. The Ouachitas are home to deer, turkey, water fowl, squirrel, and coon.

◄ Lake Murray, a 5,728-acre manmade lake, welcomes water lovers as well as other outdoor enthusiasts. Elephant Rock Recreation Area offers fishing, camping, and hiking.
▲ The Spring and Neosho rivers flow into the grand "Lake of the Cherokees," the state's main electric power source. Its thirteen hundred miles of shoreline, one hundred resorts, and twenty-nine enclosed fishing docks (some heated for year-round use) are in Twin Bridges State Park.

▲ State Highway 82 crosses over an arm of Lake Tenkiller in Cherokee Landing State Park, south of Tahlequah. This lake is stocked annually with ninety-six thousand trout, along with black bass, channel catfish, white bass, and crappie. Lake Tenkiller was named in honor of a Cherokee farmer by the name of Tenkiller, whose widow and children were granted allotments along the site of the ferry.

▲ Fort Cobb, an army post, was established in 1859 on the Washita River at the present site of the town of Fort Cobb. Today, Fort Cobb State Park lake, west of Anadarko, is a popular area for viewing the brilliant colors of autumn.

▲ The Thompson House, constructed in Tahlequah Indian Territory in the 1880s, is a Queen Anne-style home listed in the National Register of Historic Places. Its design reflects the prominence and leadership of the Thompson Family.
▶ Sardis Cove lies at the west end of Sardis Lake across from the Jack Fork Mountains. The mountains were named for Jack's Fork, where the first Choctaw meeting occurred in 1834, to develop a new constitution for the tribe.

◄ Stocked with crappie and catfish, Greenleaf Lake lies in the Cookson Hills in beautiful Greenleaf Lake State Park.
▲ Illinois River, the best-known scenic river in Oklahoma, offers float trip adventures along its seventy running miles.
►► Clayton Lake State Park's 510-acres are esconced in the Kiamichi Mountains, named prior to 1830. *Kiamichi* is from the French for "horned screamer," a bird species.

▲ Near Muskogee and Tahlequah, Lake Tenkiller State Park, with 12,900 acres and 130 miles of shoreline, appeals year-round to native Oklahomans and out-of-state visitors.
▶ Black Mesa, the state's highest point at 4,973 feet, is in the northwesternmost area. It affords panoramic views of New Mexico, Colorado, and Oklahoma's Panhandle.

◄ The Ouachita National Forest scenic turnout is at the Emerald Vista Winding Stair National Forest Recreation Area on the Talimena Scenic Drive. The Ouachita Trail is a mountainous 225-mile passageway from Oklahoma's Talimena State Park to Little Rock, Arkansas. The forty-six miles in Oklahoma follows winding rivers, traverses steep slopes, and crests three-thousand-foot mountains.
▲ The Black Fork Mountain Wilderness Area, which permits no vehicles, lies in the Ouachita National Forest.

▲ Choctaw Council House, now a museum, was built in
1884 and was the Choctaw capitol until statehood in 1907.
▶ Stephans Gap forms a backdrop to Broken Bow Lake in
Hochatown State Park. In June, the Kiamichi Owa-Chito
Festival of the Forest honors the area's Choctaw Indians,
its forest heritage, and the area's industry and craftsmen.

◄ The Charons Garden Wilderness Area, in the Wichita Mountains Wildlife Refuge, preserves the ancient rugged mountain range including Mount Scott as its summit.
▲ The Historic Library is on the University of Oklahoma campus, which opened in 1892 in Norman. The University houses the eminent University of Oklahoma Press and is a leader in meteorology and energy-related disciplines.

▲ Large granite boulders, strewn as if by a giant's hand, lie near the summit of Mount Scott, the highest of the Wichita Mountains, in the Wichita Mountain Wildlife Refuge. ▶ Oklahoma is prolific with a variety of backroads. Every state park and recreation area provides road gawking and scenic vistas. This road runs below Tenkiller Ferry Dam.

◄ Lake Tenkiller State Park offers picnicking, hiking, flora, and even an island to explore. Tenkiller Ferry Dam on the Illinois River is 197 feet high and backs up the stream for 34 miles, creating more than 130 miles of lake shoreline.

▲ The people of the town of Newkirk paid cash for the construction of their courthouse, which was completed in 1926. The fountain was restored in 1990. The War Memorial on its grounds honors Kay County's veterans of World War I, World War II, Korean War, and Vietnam War.

▲ The Ferguson Home in Watonga was constructed in 1901 by Thomas Benton Ferguson. Territorial Governor of Oklahoma from 1901 to 1905, Ferguson's term of office came to an end just two years before Oklahoma became a state, in 1907. The building is now open to the public.

▲ Lake Altus (also called Lugert Lake) in Quartz Mountain State Park has some 6,260 surface acres, forty-nine-miles of shoreline, excellent fishing, and abundant vegetation.
►► This medieval-style fortress located in Ardmore was intended to be a state governors' retreat, but it hovered—unfinished and unused—over Lake Murrray until 1950, when the building was converted to a nature center. Now a museum, it displays one of the largest meterorites in the world along with numerous fossils and wildlife exhibits.

▲ In northwest Oklahoma, south of the Cimarron River, these red buttes, referred to as either the Gloss Mountains or the Glass Mountains, thrill far-away gapers with their earthy tones and the sparkly crystals covering their slopes.

▲ Lake Murray and Lake Murray State Park was named after Governor William H. "Alfalfa Bill" Murray, who served from 1931 to 1935. His son, Johnston Murray, also was governor from 1951 to 1955. This is Oklahoma's—and perhaps the nation's—only father-son governor team.

▲ Oklahoma City celebrates the Arts Festival each April with concerts on Pond Stage performed by singers and other musicians and with artists and international cuisine.
▶ Quanah Park Lake sparkles like a jewel in the Wichita Mountains Wildlife Refuge. A visitor center provides orientation exhibits and other information about the area.

◄ Emerald Vista is just one of the many outstanding view spots on the Winding Stair Mountain on the Talimena Scenic Drive in Ouachita National Forest. Hunting in the Ouachitas is divided into rifle, musket, and bow seasons.
▲ The Cimarron River follows its valley the length of the Panhandle, cutting across the northwest ridge of the state.